Boats
and Ships

Angela Royston

Illustrated by
John Downes

Contents

First published in Great Britain in 1997 by Heinemann Children's Reference,
an imprint of Heinemann Educational Publishers, Halley Court, Jordan Hill, Oxford, OX2 8EJ,
a division of Reed Educational & Professional Publishing Ltd.

MADRID ATHENS PRAGUE WARSAW FLORENCE PORTSMOUTH NH
CHICAGO SAO PAULO SINGAPORE TOKYO MEXICO MELBOURNE
AUCKLAND IBADAN GABORONE JOHANNESBURG KAMPALA NAIROBI

© Reed Educational & Professional Publishing Ltd, 1997

ISBN 0 431 06540 3

British Library Cataloguing in Publication Data
Royston, Angela, First look through boats and ships
1. Boats and boating - Juvenile literature 2. Ships - Juvenile literature
I. Title II. Boats and ships 623.8'2

Photo credits: page 7: © ZEFA; page 9, 14 and 21: © J. Allan Cash Ltd; page 11: © ZEFA-DEUTER;
page 12: FLPA © T Whittaker; page 13: Britstock-IFA © Eve Klein; page 19: Tony Stone Worldwide © David Higgs; page 22: © TRH/Royal Navy.

Editor: Alyson Jones
Designer: Peter Clayman
Picture Researcher: Liz Eddison
Art Director: Cathy Tincknell
Production Controller: Lorraine Stebbing

Printed and bound in Italy.
See-through pages printed by SMIC, France.

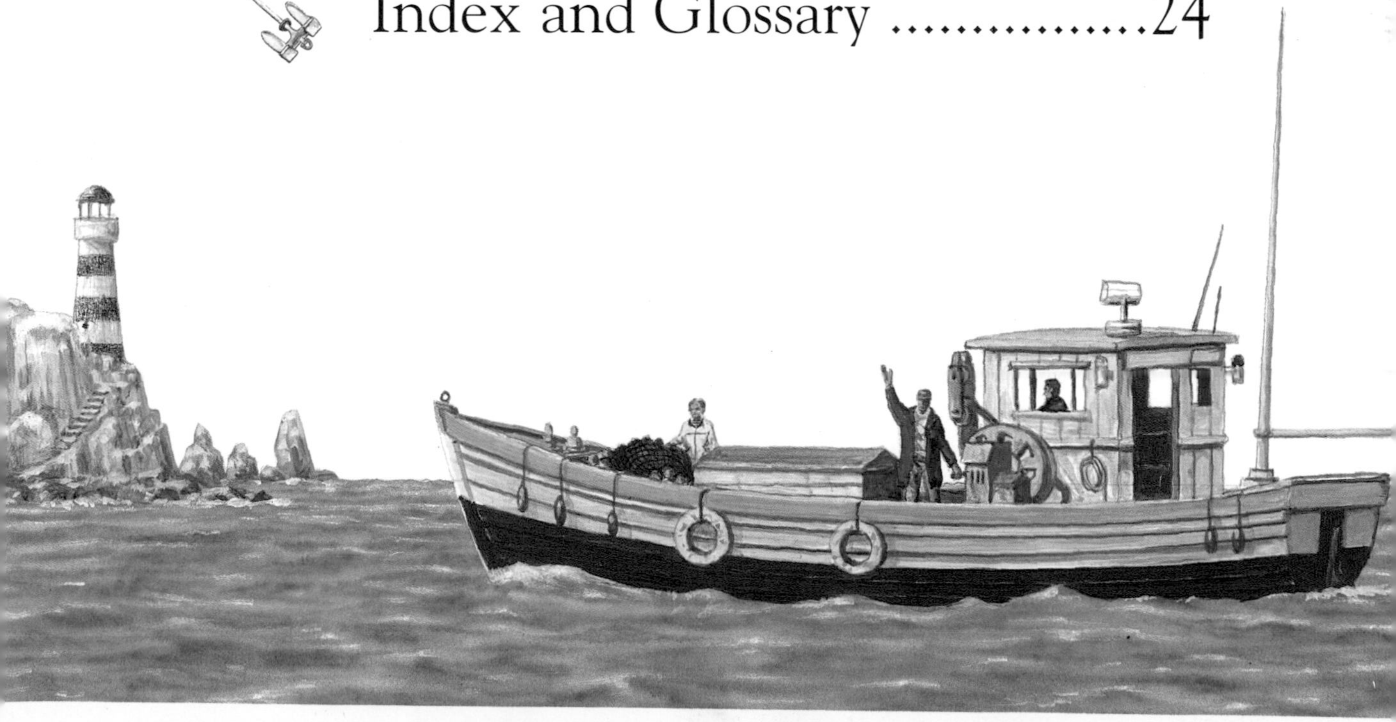

Boating for Fun

People use boats to travel or to carry things across water. Many people also sail boats just for fun. Can you see the speedboat pulling a water-skier? Windsurfers cut through the water, but they are not as fast as the speedboat!

A cabin cruiser is like a floating home. It has seats and bunk beds inside. Just right for a holiday on the water!

The person inside this canoe is wearing a helmet and a lifejacket in case it is tipped over by the strong waves.

Carrying Cargo

Cargo ships carry things from place to place – even halfway around the world! Oil tankers are the biggest cargo ships. Underneath the long deck are huge tanks full of oil. Look how small the tug looks next to the tanker!

These boats carry a different kind of cargo. They belong to farmers in Southeast Asia. The farmers paddle down the river to sell their vegetables.

At the Port

There is a lot to see in a busy port. A red tug is pulling a container ship into the port. An orange crane is unloading large containers from another ship. Only one container fits onto a truck!

The harbour on the right shelters smaller boats. How many boats can you count in the harbour?

Look at all the boats
packed into this small
harbour in Greece. It is so
full the boats have to tie
up close together.

Sailing Boats

In some parts of the world, sailing boats are still used for fishing or to carry cargo. People also sail boats for fun. The wind catches the sails and blows the boat along. The stronger the wind blows, the faster the boat goes!

These yachts are in a race. The crew lean far back to balance the sails. Can you see one person on each boat moving the rudder? This steers the boat. The other person hauls in the sails.

This Chinese sailing boat is called a junk. It is made of wood and has linen sails. Even though it looks old, it is a very strong, safe boat.

For hundreds of years, people have sailed across the oceans in boats like this. Sailors climb up the masts to take in the sails.

Ferries

Ferries sail at certain times each day or week. The biggest ferries carry cars, buses and trucks, as well as people. A big door at the front of the ferry rises up and the vehicles drive straight on.

This ferry in Guyana carries goods and people. Can you see what it has unloaded?

In India people cross from the island of Goa to the mainland on a small ferry. These people rush up the slipway to go to work.

Skimming the Waves

Hydrofoils and hovercraft are used to speed people from one island to another, across lakes and even across the sea. As a hydrofoil moves forward, the wings underneath it push down on the water and raise the boat up.

A hovercraft can travel over flat land as well as water. It moves on a cushion of air which is trapped beneath the hovercraft.

Hydrofoils skim over the water on underwater wings.

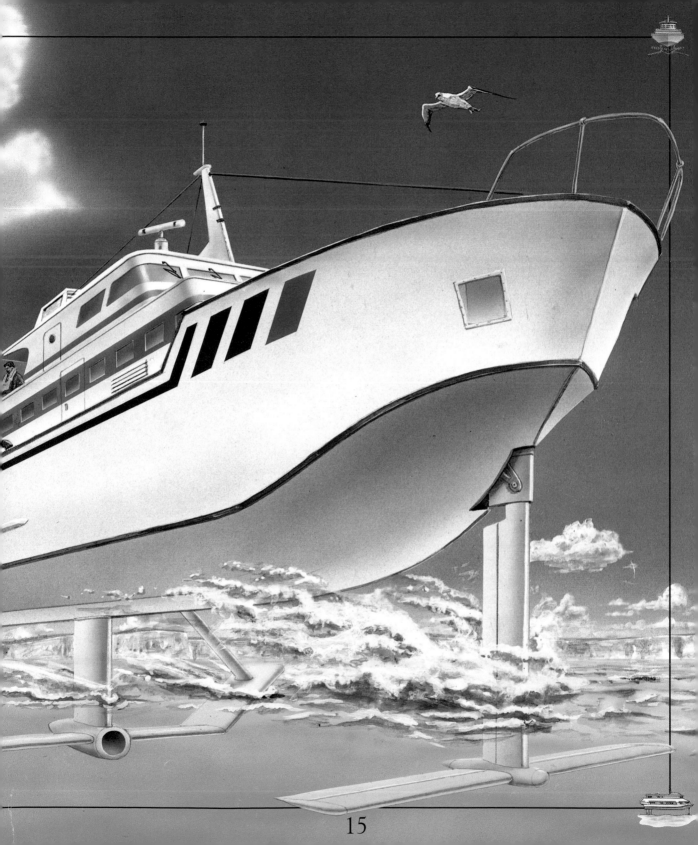

Fishing Boats

We are off for a day's fishing. Can you see the nets that will be used to catch the fish? The fisherman in the small boat will lower pots down to the seabed. He hopes lobsters and crabs will scuttle into the pots!

This African fisherman throws a large net over the fish and pulls them in. The poles on the other side of the canoe stop it tipping over.

Bigger fishing boats can stay at sea for several weeks. The biggest boats have huge freezers on board to keep the fish fresh.

Soon the crew of the fishing
boat will pull in their net full
of fish. Who else is hoping to
catch a fish today?

Under the Sea

Small submarines are called submersibles. They travel thousands of metres down into the depths of the sea. Submersibles are used to inspect and mend pipes and cables under the sea. Others are used to explore the seabed or shipwrecks.

This submersible does not have people inside. It uses video cameras to send pictures back to a ship on the surface of the sea.

Can you see the diver? She is
getting ready to explore
outside this submersible.

The biggest submarines
are warships. They can
stay underwater for
months at a time, but
they can also sail on
the surface.

Cruising Ships

Cruise ships are like floating hotels. Passengers sleep in cabins and spend their holiday sailing from place to place across tropical seas. There are plenty of things to do on board. Some people swim in the swimming pools on the deck.

Large lifeboats hang at the sides of the cruise ship.

Paddle-steamers used to carry cargo and passengers up and down the Mississippi river in the United States. This one now carries tourists.

This small cruise boat takes tourists on a tour of the canals of Amsterdam in Holland. Lots of other boats travel on these canals.

Warships

The biggest warships are aircraft carriers. They are floating airports for warplanes. The planes can land and refuel on the aircraft carrier and then return to duty.

This destroyer can fire guided missiles to protect itself from submarines and aircraft. A computer guides the missile to its target.

Pilots need a lot of skill to make their planes take off and land on the moving deck. They must not miss the runway!

Index

Glossary

Cabin   a small room in a ship

Container   a large box in which cargo (goods) is stored

Crew   a team of people who work together on a boat

Deck   the floor on a ship

Freezer   a machine that keeps things inside it cold

Lifejacket   a special vest made of material that helps you float in water

Mast   a long pole that holds up the ship's sails

Paddle-steamer   a boat that is moved by paddles turned by steam

Rudder   an object fixed to the back of a boat that is used to steer it

Slipway   a slope down to water

Windsurfer   someone who rides a sailboard, a simple board with a sail